MUMBAI MONOCHROME

photos and haiku

MUMBAI MONOCHROME

photos and haiku

Suhit Kelkar

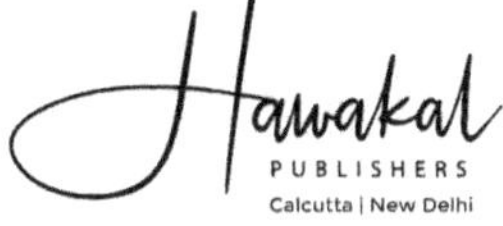

Hawakal
PUBLISHERS
Calcutta | New Delhi

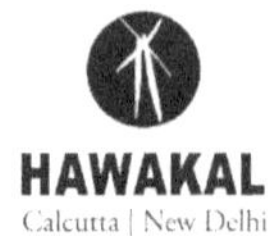

HAWAKAL PUBLISHERS
33/1/2 K B Sarani, Mall Road, Calcutta 80
70-B/9 Amritpuri, East of Kailash, New Delhi 65

Email info@hawakal.com
Website www.hawakal.com

Cover art by Arunangshu Roy
Cover designed by Bitan Chakraborty

First edition: December 2020

Copyright 2020 © Suhit Kelkar

ISBN: 978-81-948538-7-9

Price: INR 350 | USD 10.99

UNSPOKEN REALIZATIONS

Photographers often say that the best camera is the one you have with you when you want to take a photo. For most of us, that is the camera on our mobile phone. Speaking of myself: while the mobile phone camera hasn't replaced my 'serious' camera, it works well in many situations involving my chosen genre, which is street photography. I find that mobile phone cameras have advanced to the point where they suffice for my work: they produce large enough files for social media, and given their fairly high resolution, the photos they produce can be printed in reasonably large sizes. Autofocus tech has advanced to the point where even mobile phone cameras record moments that draw my attention to street life, including moderately fast action; and produce clear photos even in fairly low light. Innovations in imaging tech have automated most of the technical aspects of photography, leaving me free to focus on the art of it—the composition, the meaning-making, the other aspects that turn a scene or situation into a photo. Of course, there are also times when the camera gets its settings wrong. That is where my training as a photographer comes in. I can always adjust the setting that needs to be changed. But most times I don't have to fret about every setting.

All but three or four of the photos in this book were taken with mobile phone cameras. When it was necessary, I used manual mode. Usually though, there wasn't time to fiddle with camera settings, and I left the mobile phone camera in auto mode for fear of losing the moment. When I use my 'serious' camera (a Fujifilm XE_3 with a 23mm $F_2.0$ lens, in case you were wondering) I put it in Aperture Priority, also selecting the ISO but leaving the shutter speed and White Balance in Auto mode. When using the Fuji, moreover, I turn autofocus off and prefer to use zone focusing using the in-camera distance scale. This way saves the precious fraction of a moment that would be lost in autofocusing.

I know that my statements won't be liked by those who conflate full manual control of a camera with artistic merit. Manual control alone does not make a photographer. It is necessary on many occasions, but it does not suffice—you must also have a good eye. That is where technology has not replaced the photographer. Not yet, anyway.

A couple of months back, I posted a photo (that is not a part of this book) to the popular website named *Reddit*. The photo was liked by a number of people there; what lodged itself in my mind, though, was the comment of a Redditor, who said my gaze was that of an alien who was roaming Mumbai in his UFO. The comment struck me as rude, but also perceptive; though made perhaps in an offhand mood, it hit home with me, and made me introspect. As a few days passed, I grudgingly saw the insight in the statement. It struck me that I am in fact particularly attuned to the strangeness of mundane life. Or perhaps, the strangeness lies not out there, but in my gaze and perspective, which makes the familiar look unfamiliar, recontextualizing it, or removing context for the most part. There is, of course, more to my work than that, as there is to any photographer's work. But the fundamental point made by the Redditor stands. My photography underlines the strange in the everyday, the unfamiliar in the familiar, as if I were looking at it for the first time. Isn't it one of the functions of art to spur you to look at the everyday world with a new gaze? If that is what I've succeeded in doing through my photography, I consider myself fortunate.

That is the crux of my practice, but if I said I had it all figured out, I'd be lying. No doubt there are facets of my photographic gaze that are, if not instinctive, then at least approaching that state. For me, photography is an unpredictable alchemy of a particular photographic gaze, insight, training, the fluid situation, as well as the characteristics of the camera. The combined weight of biology, psychology, technology, and culture presses the shutter button.

Please correct me if I'm wrong in saying no photographic practice is wholly conscious or even wholly intentional. Sometimes, when I take a photo, I know I want to keep it. But sometimes I take a photograph, review it on the LCD, and do not want to delete it, but also don't want to keep it. I take another photograph, then another, and the earlier photo that gave me an ambivalent feeling is forgotten as I slip through the tunnel of the ever-shifting present. Then, when my photographic trip has ended and I go home and review my crop of photos, I discover that I like that photo. It finds a place in my heart because it speaks to me. But my photo-making is more of a chronicle of the unspoken and half-recognized events taking place inside my head at that moment, the longings, the unspoken realizations, the alignment of feelings. The photo has given a shape to the shapeless in my head. It whispers to me in my own private language. And all this happened in the few moments it took for me to recognize the image in real time. How could this process be wholly conscious? I am not claiming that any mystical factors collude in my photo-making, only psychological compulsions. But the psychological events within oneself are not wholly known to one, for whatever reason.

If taking a photo is, as I've claimed, not entirely a conscious process for me, then photo editing is its opposite. It is on the editing computer (as I do not shoot film) that my conscious mind, more than my unconscious mind, plays with the potential of the photo. Even then, in editing my photos, I am building upon the groundwork that was, after all, laid by ineffable impulses. Editing serves to accentuate in the photo what my impulse was drawn to outside it. On the editing screen, even a reticent photo reveals the impulse that lay behind it.

I am an accidental photographer. While growing up, I showed no promise as a photographer, on the few occasions when I got film cameras, both point-and-shoot and SLR, to use. What I lacked in ability and training I made up for with my enthusiasm to take photos. It was only as an adult that I picked up a camera with serious intent.

Of course, a way of seeing the world may come from various inputs that are not entirely susceptible to training, namely the psychological, but it is through wisdom and training that this way of seeing is honed. Do excuse me if I do not dwell on the wellsprings beneath my yearning to make images, whether through text or the camera. In part the yearning stems from personal psychology, of course, but perhaps also from a universal human urge to see, to remember, to memorialise, to make sense, to frame aesthetically, and to be present in the living moment. Many excellent scholars have theorized about the general human urge to take photos. I want this essay to be personal.

My path towards photography began with journalism. In 2001, I began my career as a news reporter. In the newsroom, I found myself drawn more to photojournalists I worked with than to fellow reporters. The reporters wrote well, but did not make good conversation about things that interested me. The photographers, meanwhile, had their Fellowship of the Image, that look in their eye, and I found myself listening in on their discussions on making beauty or at least meaning out of the mundane. I listened to them and began looking at award-winning and famous photographic work online. And of course, I became friends with photojournalist colleagues because we covered assignments together. I saw them work, and was fascinated as they combined intent with intuition. I was hooked to their art, as a rasik.

I had worked six or seven years and had then quit as a staff reporter, when I bought my first camera, the Nikon D3100 model DSLR. I had quit jobs because I was sick of the routine nature of daily newspapering, as well as its penchant for specializing in disasters and tragedies. I was also in poor mental health. For more reasons than one, I wanted out of newspaper work. I wanted a change. Aflame with the appeal of the telling image, I thought I would become a photographer.

So, in order to acquire another income-generating skill, I took a photography course in my hometown, Mumbai. The course reinforced the idea that taking photos was an art, and to learn the intricacies of the photographic art, its historical, technological, aesthetic and practical aspects. I began taking photos, and taking them seriously. My photographic equipment changed, and I kept improving as a photographer, even if I say so myself. I actually did a few freelance assignments as a photographer, but did not enjoy the commercial aspect of that work. I returned to freelance journalistic writing—this time round, writing on arts and culture—as a means of livelihood. But I never lost my appetite for photography. It became a purely creative pursuit. You can call it a hobby—a term used for anything that is seldom sold, no matter how seriously it is done.

My practice as a poet has infected my photographic practice. Photography and poetry are distinct arts, but there is a lot of overlap between them, at least there is, in the way I see them. To my mind, a good stanza and a good photograph are both strange and silent: they defamiliarize, which accounts for their strangeness; and they communicate as much through the associations and implications they throw up, as through their overt content; or they should.

The photographs in this book depict moments from everyday life, moments that are small rather than momentous, mundane rather than dramatic. They are mostly quiet moments—

I am drawn to them because they are rare events in a city like Mumbai, which is usually noisy and overcrowded. That alone does not, however, make these photos notable in my eyes. One, they have some quality that unifies disparate elements in the frame into a cohesive whole – whether colours that work together, certain aligned visual elements, or themes whether visual or conceptual or emotional. That is true of any photo. But there is more that makes a photo in my eye—usually it is a universality or general-ness about a scene, which lifts it up from the everyday, and a storytelling potential.

In this book the photos are accompanied by haiku, three-line poems that have been described by historian George Sansom as 'drops of poetic essence.' I take issue with the word 'essence.' However one defines them, many of these haiku contain a central image (here, I mean an image which is constructed with words), then play with it, juxtaposing it with another image or insight that induces a recontextualization of that image. In this book, each haiku is paired up with a photo. So each haiku also plays with the accompanying photo, and hopefully adds a layer to each photo that enriches your pleasure at having viewed it.

Thank you first and foremost for buying this book. I am also thankful to the enterprising folks at *Hawakal*—Bitan Chakraborty and Kiriti Sengupta, for their enthusiastic backing of this project. On a personal note, I am thankful to my parents for unstintingly supporting my desire to become an artist. Thanks to my friends, who have encouraged my poetic and photographic practice. And thanks to Dr. Milan Balakrishnan, who enabled me to live a life that is largely free of mental suffering.

I hope you enjoy this book.

Thank you.

Suhit Kelkar
Mumbai

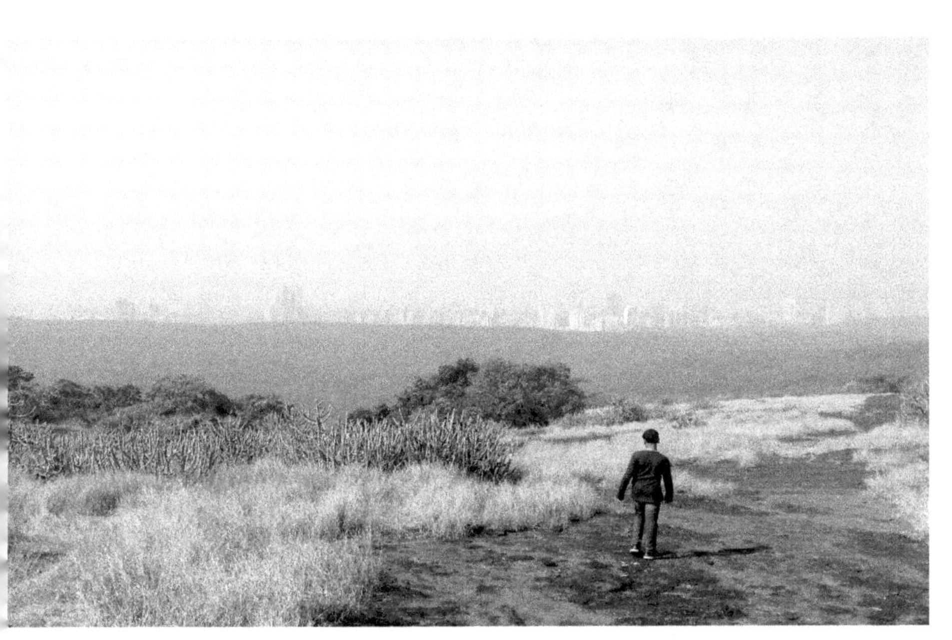

crossroads
I wait for the cool wind
to go first

children's sandals
headed nowhere
my bloodline

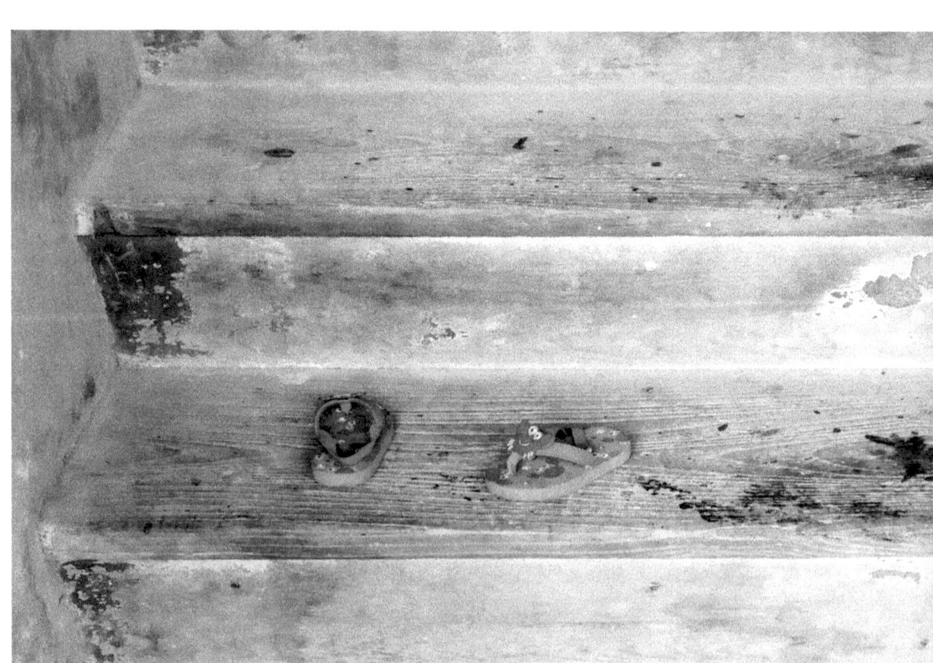

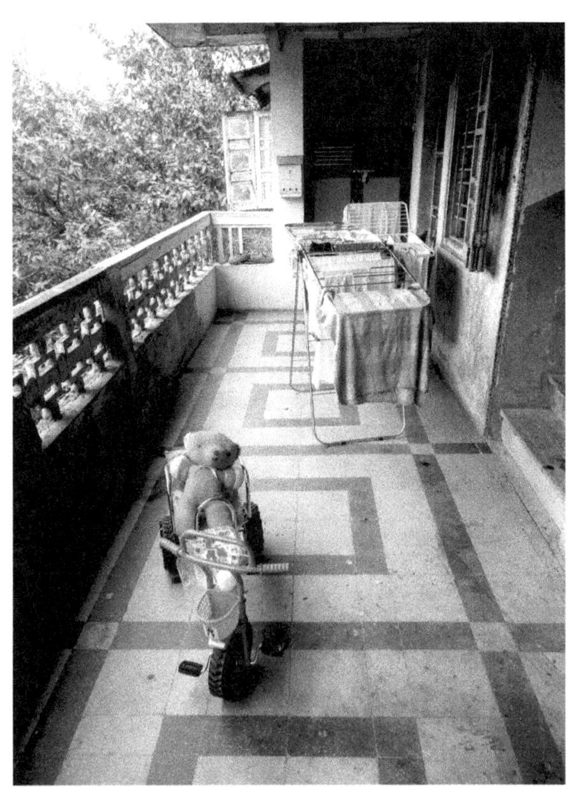

nap time
the plush bear waits
for his friends

doll's dreams
the deserted street
unfolds

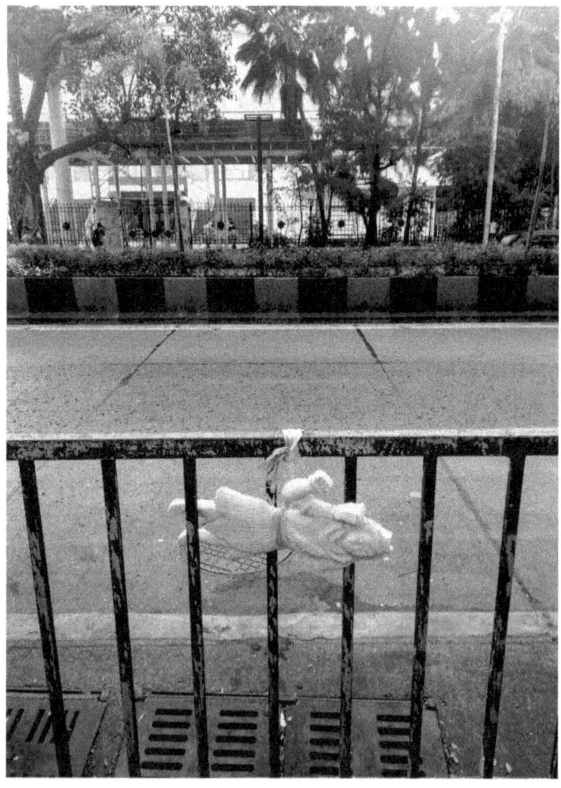

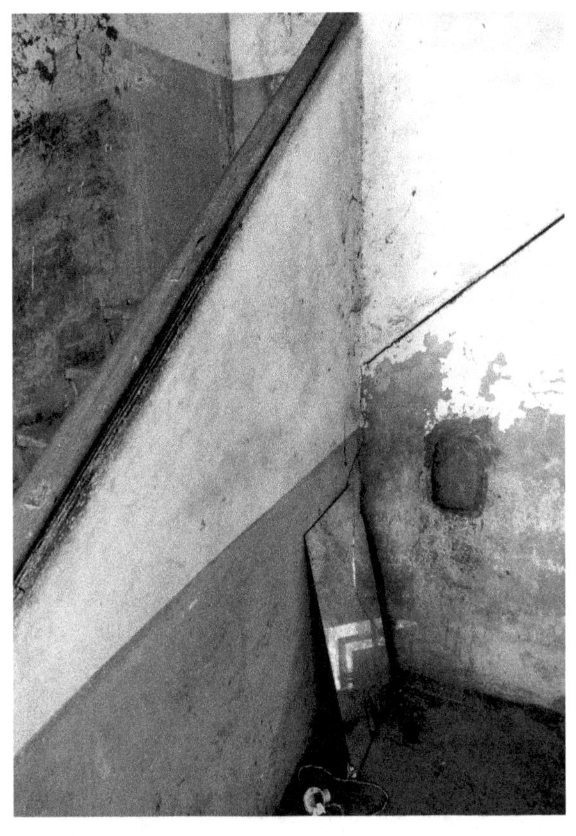

cracked mirror
the patina
of leaked reflections

razor gleam
shadows peeled
from his cheek

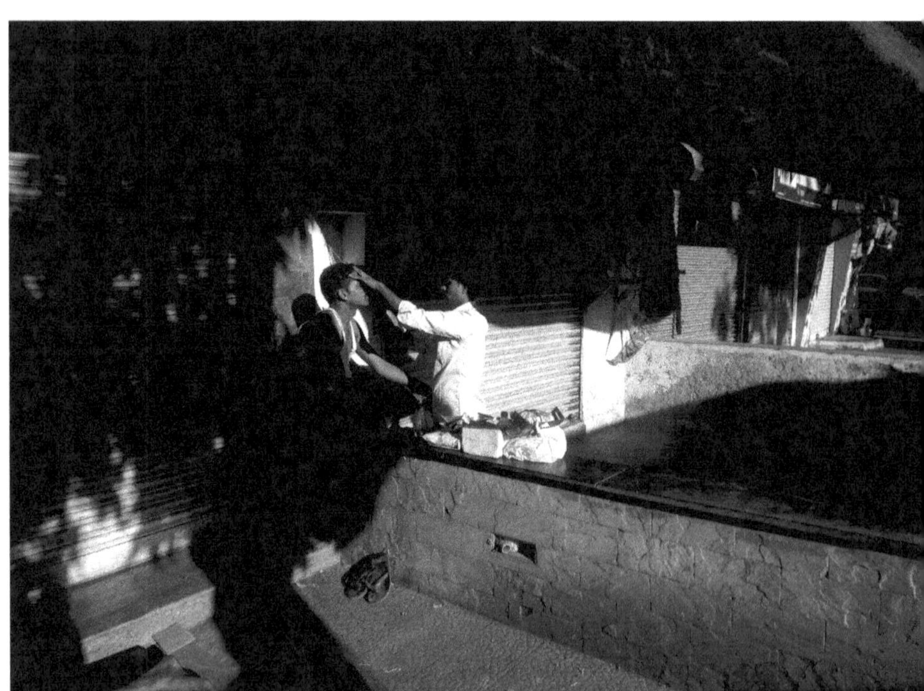

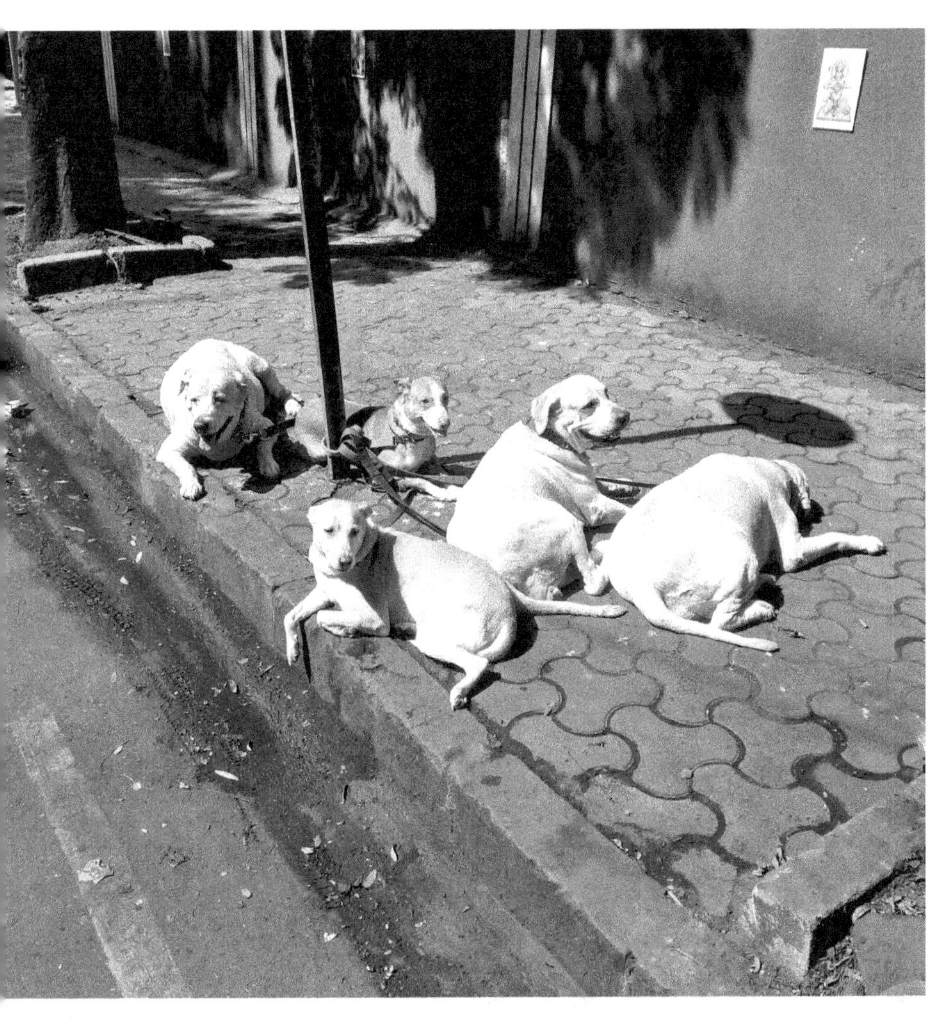

the dog's leash
in its own mouth
I recall my obsessions

afternoon
the feeder slaked
without eating

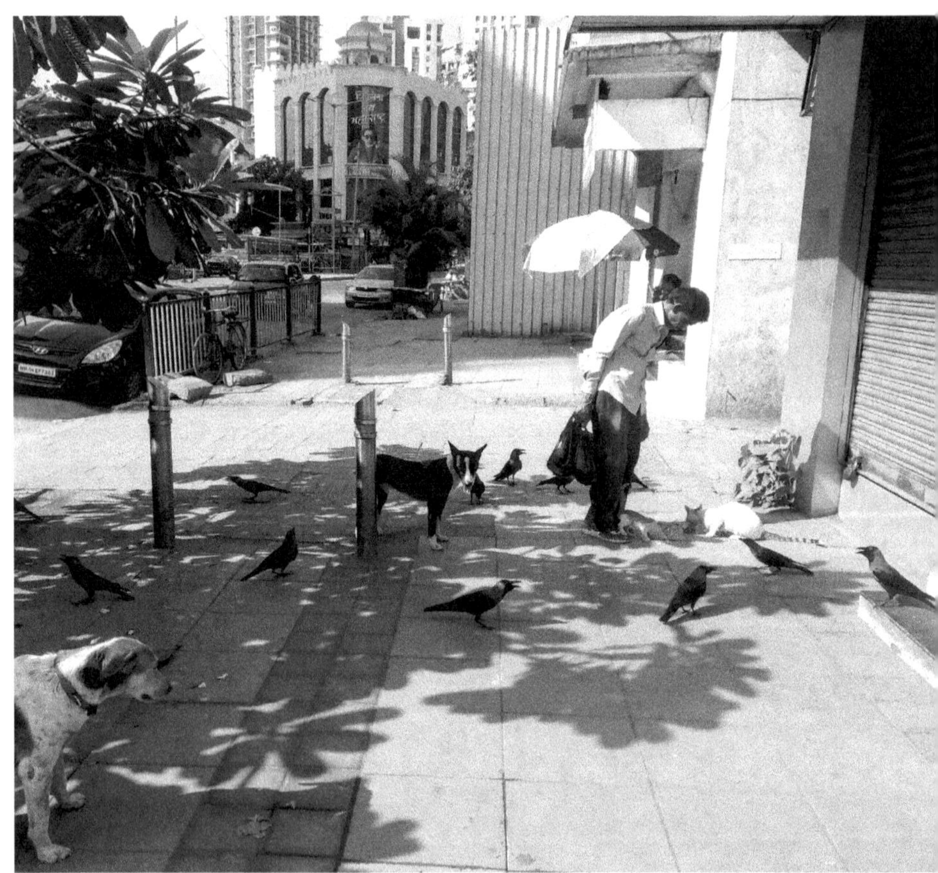

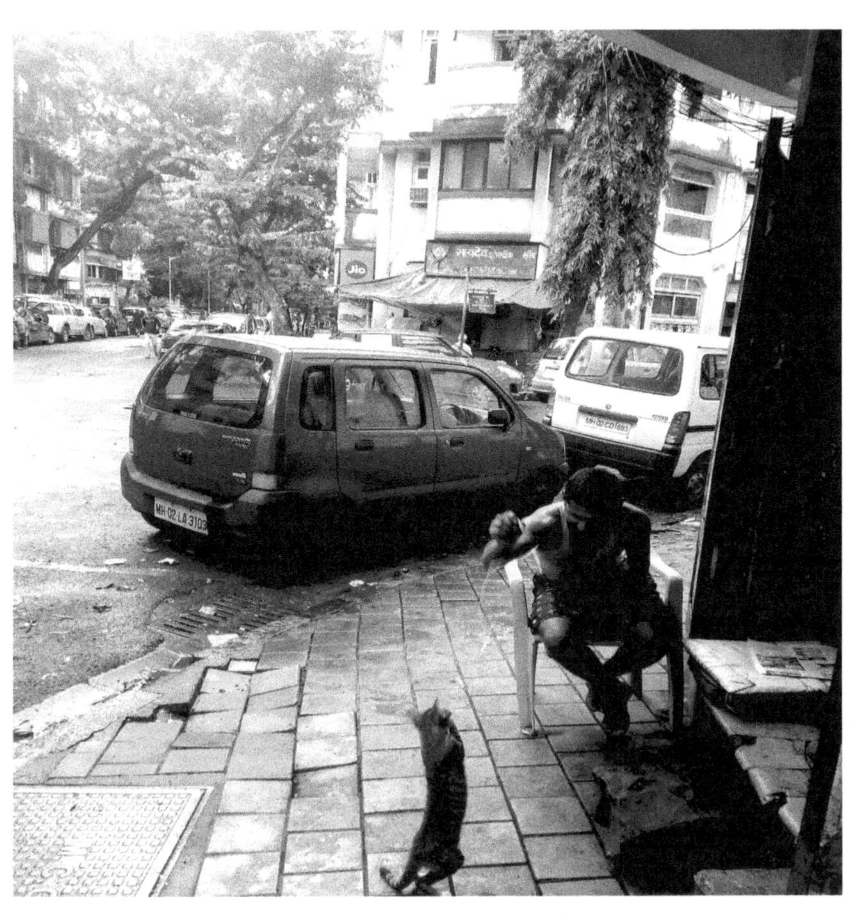

cat's eye
a moment as long
as a dancing string

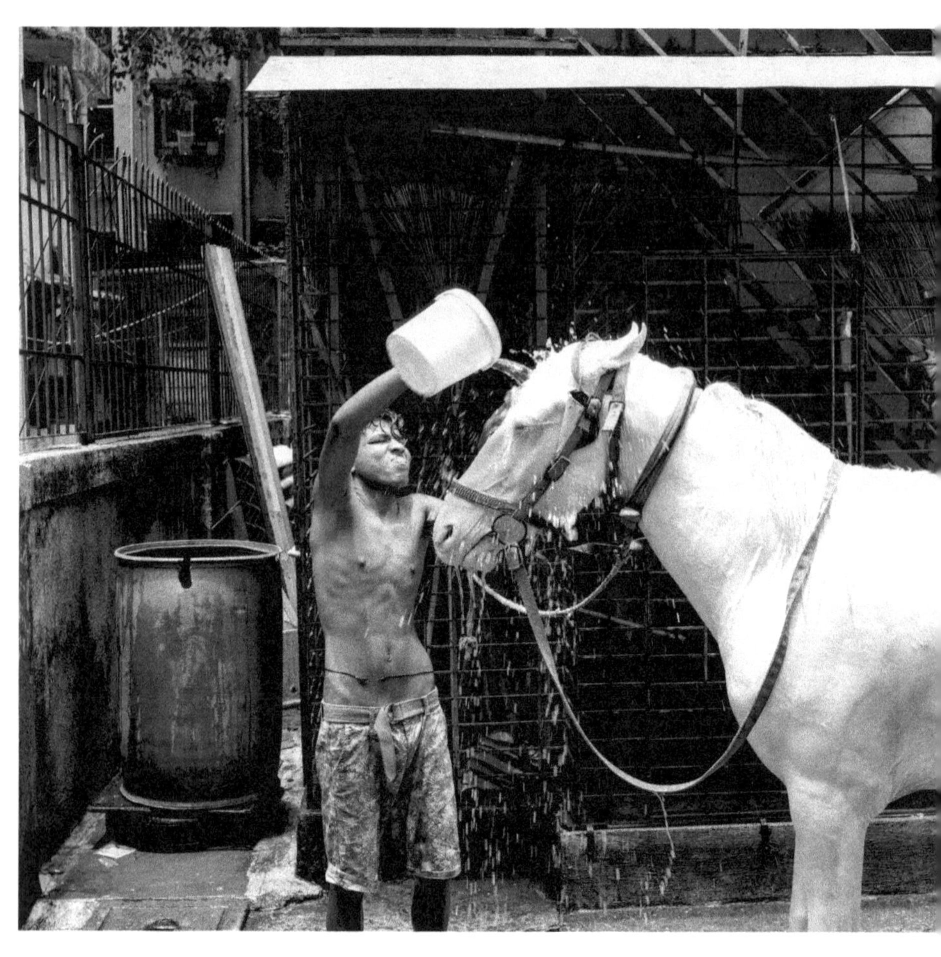

after wedding season
cool water douses
the horse's memories

missing having
a pet at my heels
noonday shadow

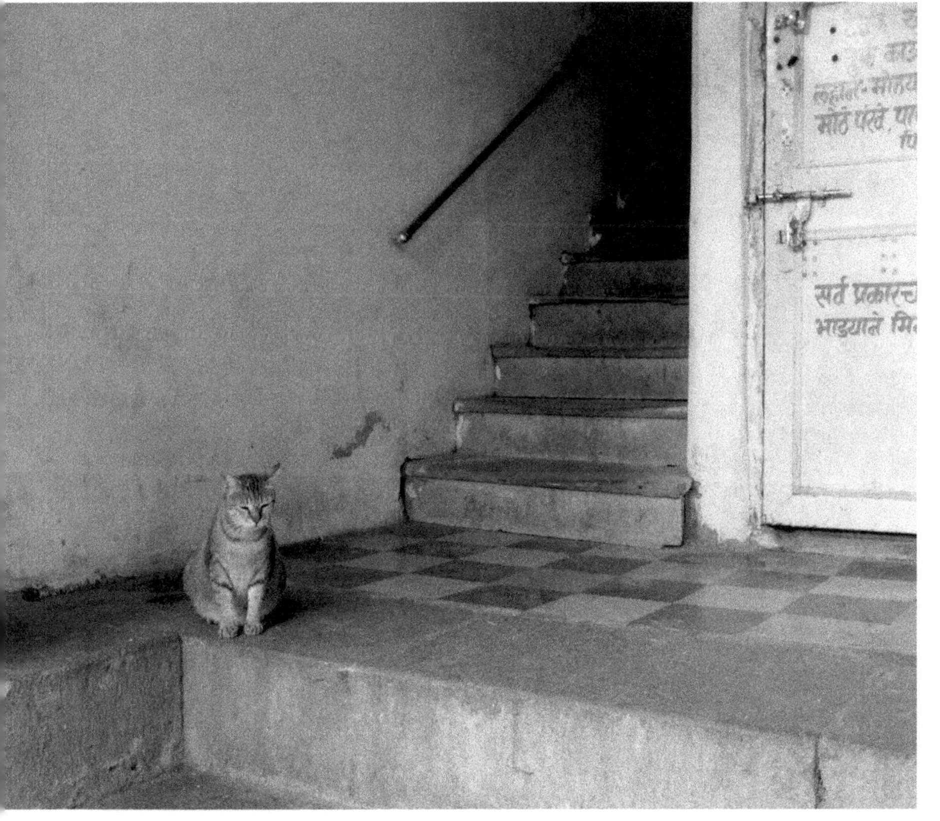

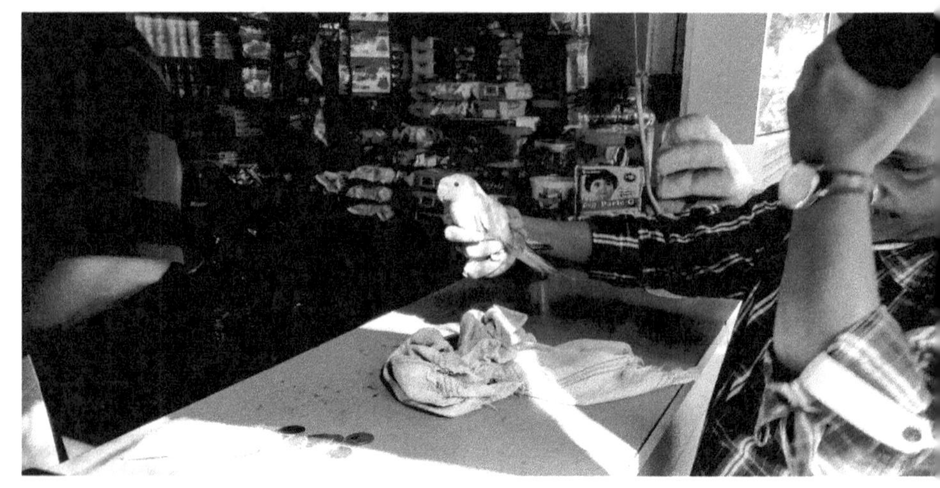

after cliché
comes compassion –
fallen fledgling

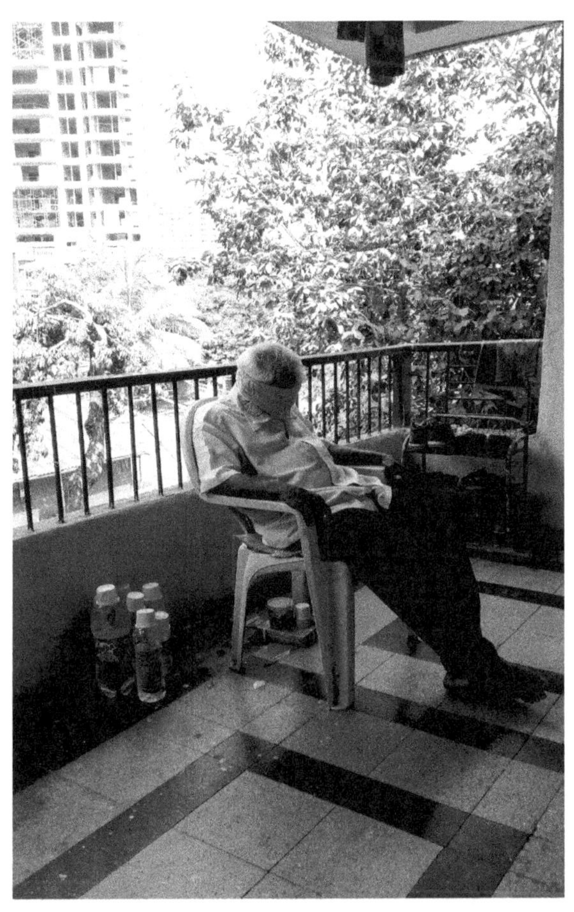

blindfold
yet a dream
keeps him awake

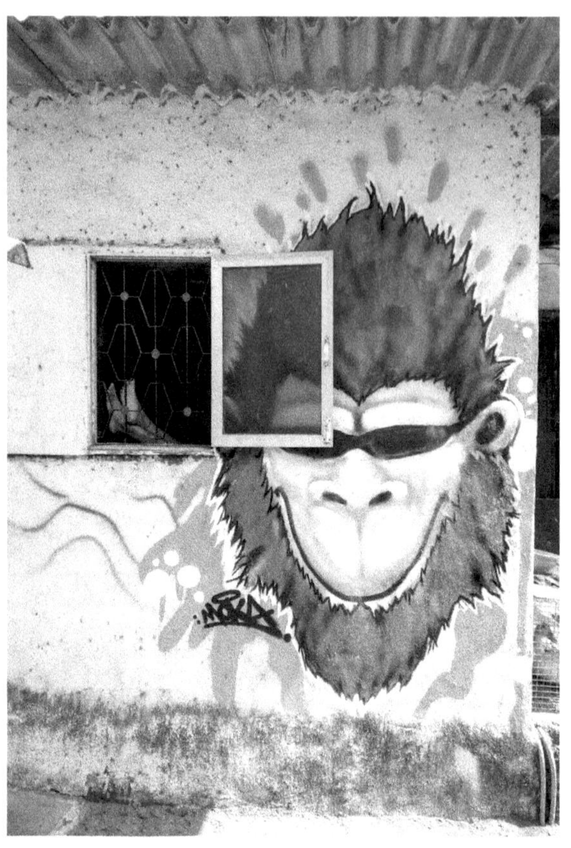

winks with his right
winks with his left
the dream unbroken

fairground
empty mirrors
await new mirages

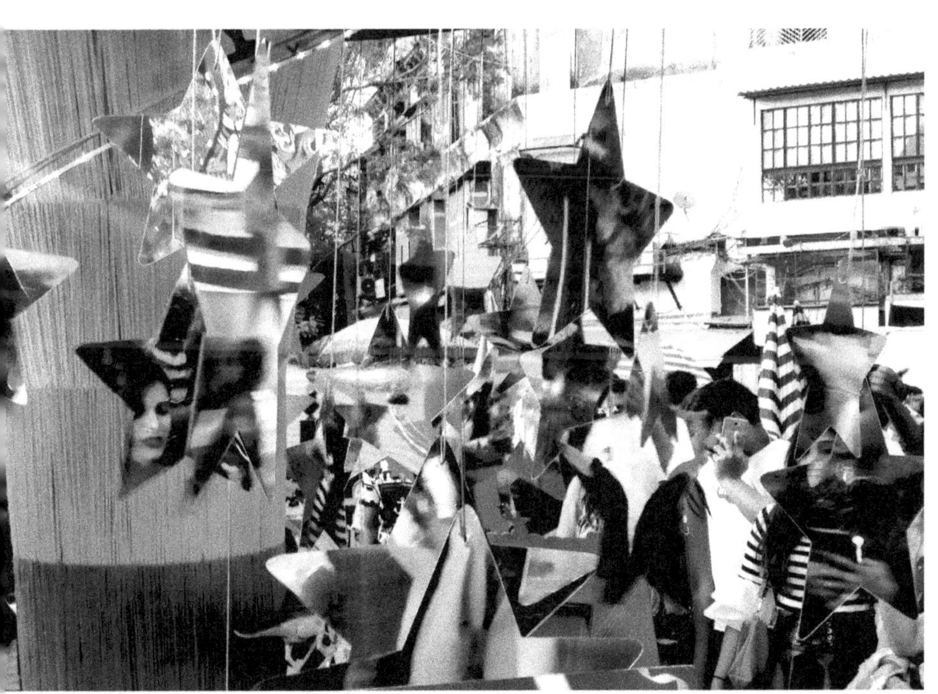

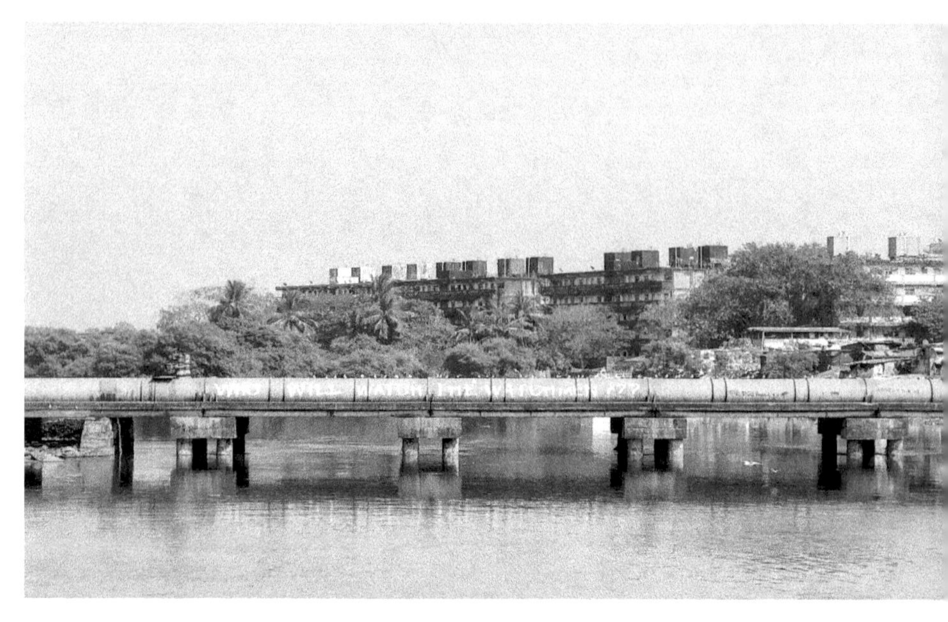

peeling but legible
dissent
outlasts the monsoon

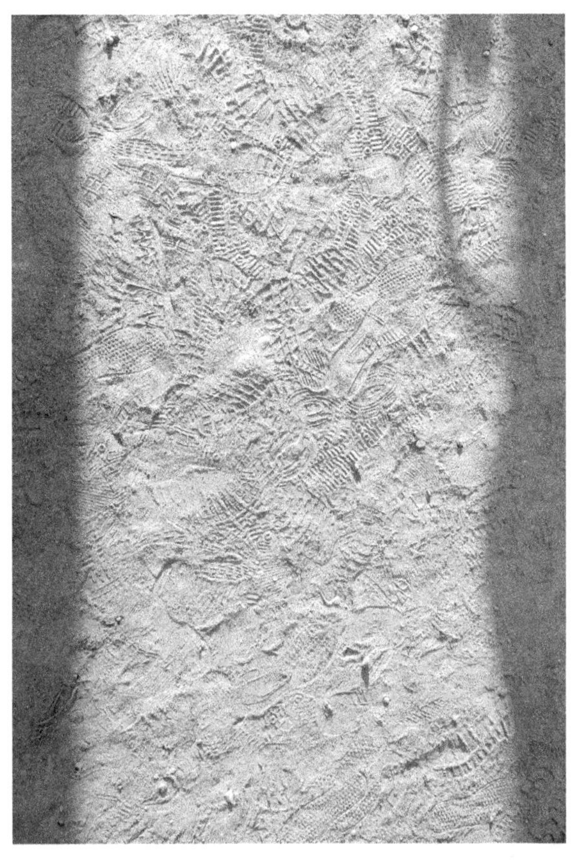

seeking a new poem
I look down
someone else's footsteps

not yet holy
white crosses
await customers

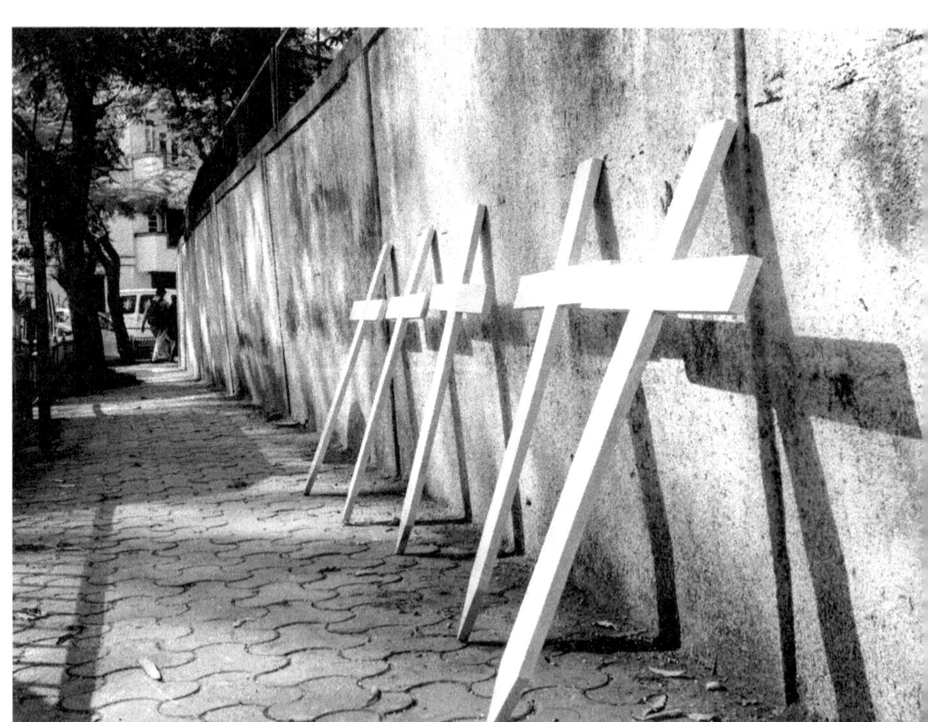

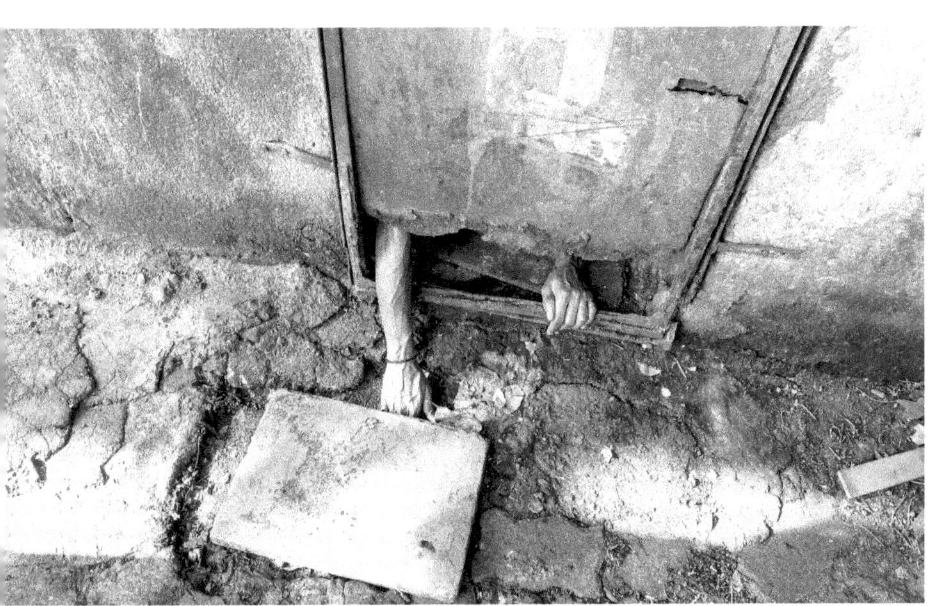

disembodied hands
those branches
that I pruned

seller of sweets
a trunk full
of memories

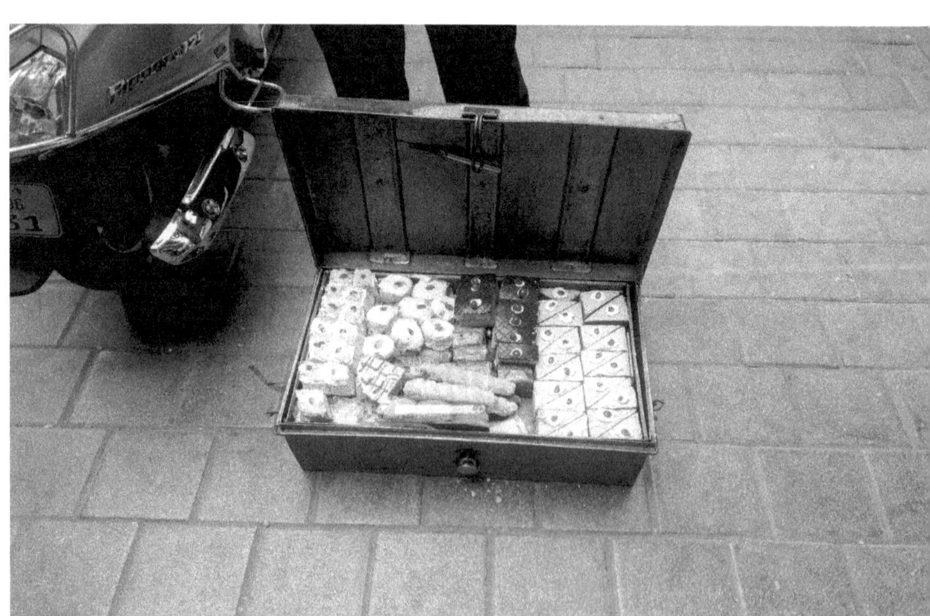

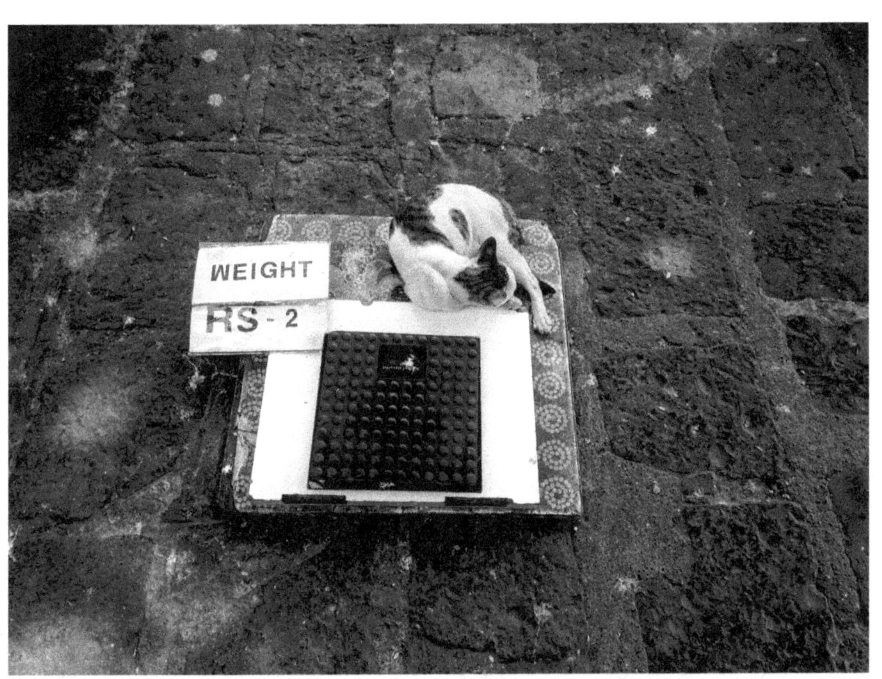

all the Tindering
that I have skipped
weighing scale

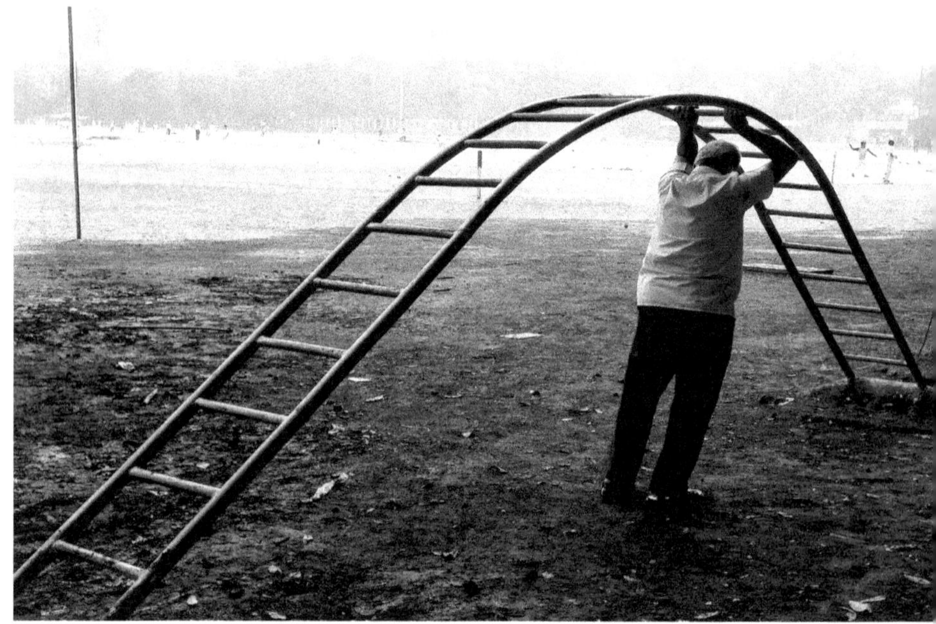

morning exercise
one day
I too will be old

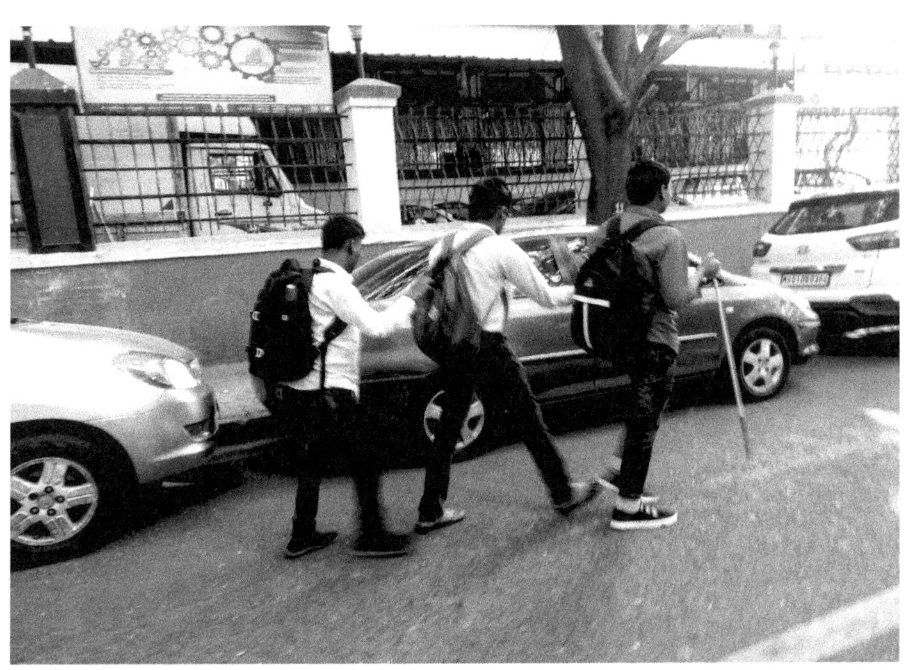

India
three blind men
and no elephant

evening
the sun's light
forms a haiku

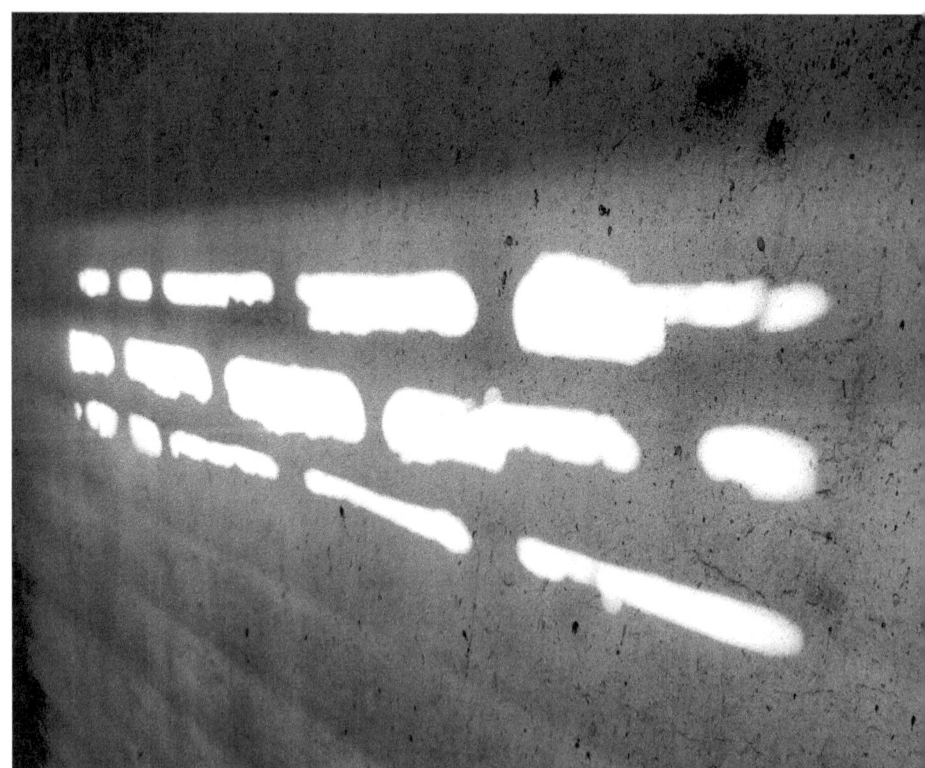

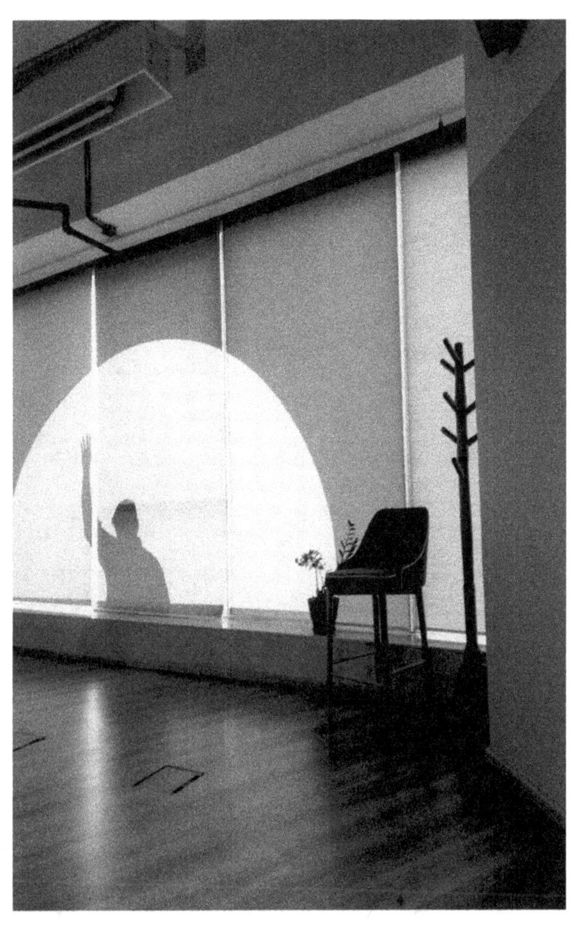

makeup removal
his gestures
unravel him

flour mill
my yearning for snow
deepens

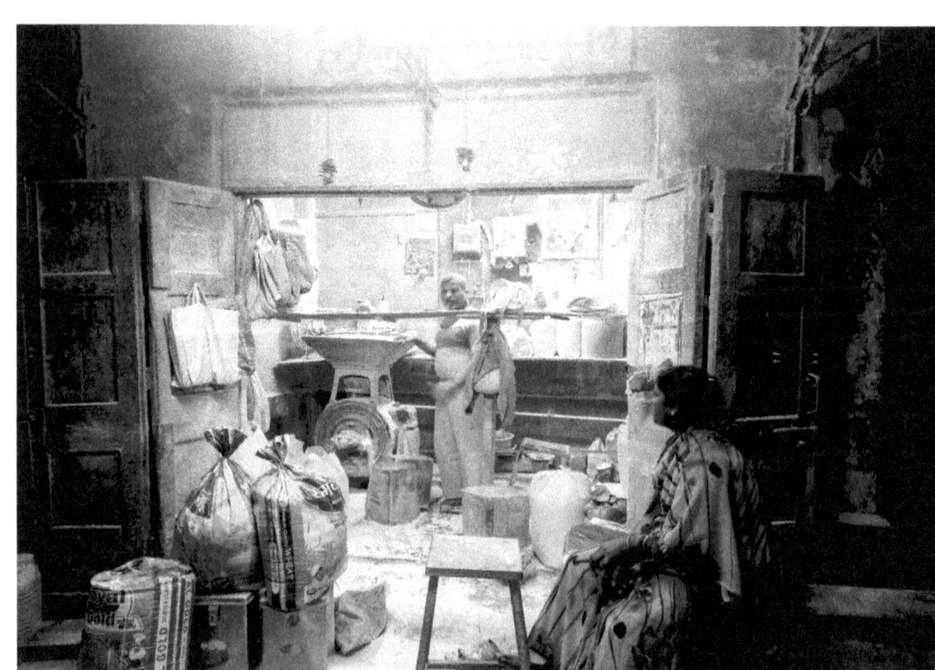

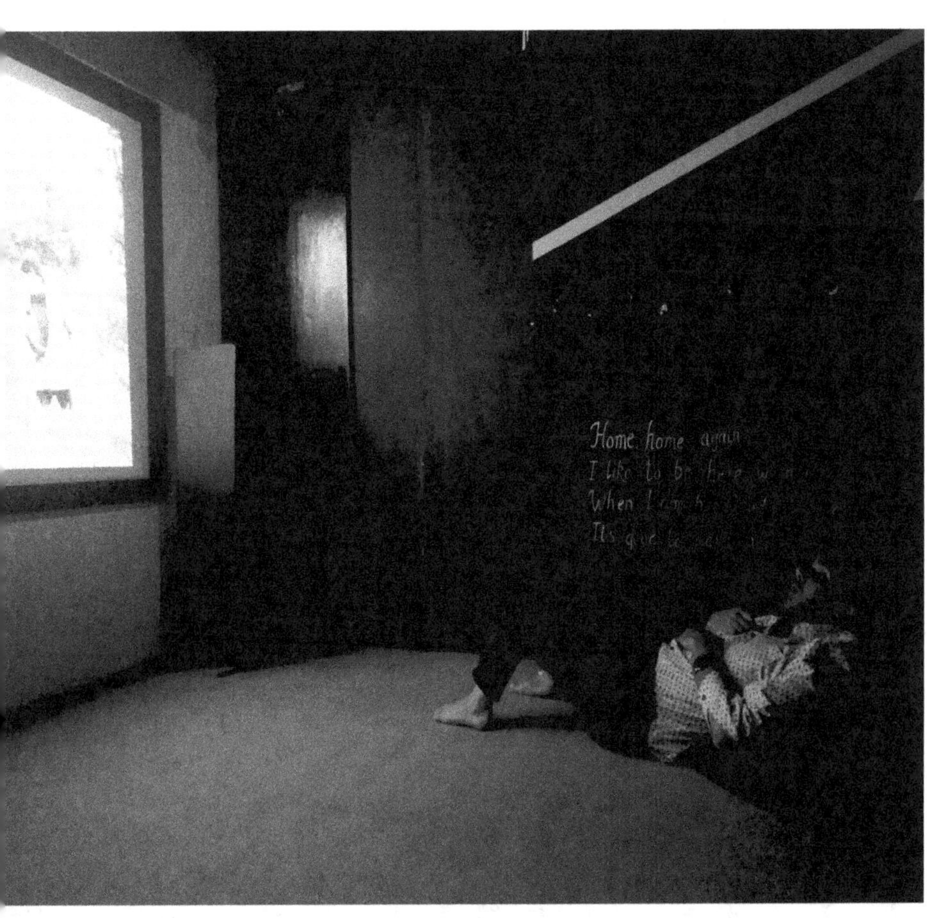

morning
yesterday's movie
still tints his cheek

vinyl session
purple notes
in murmuring light

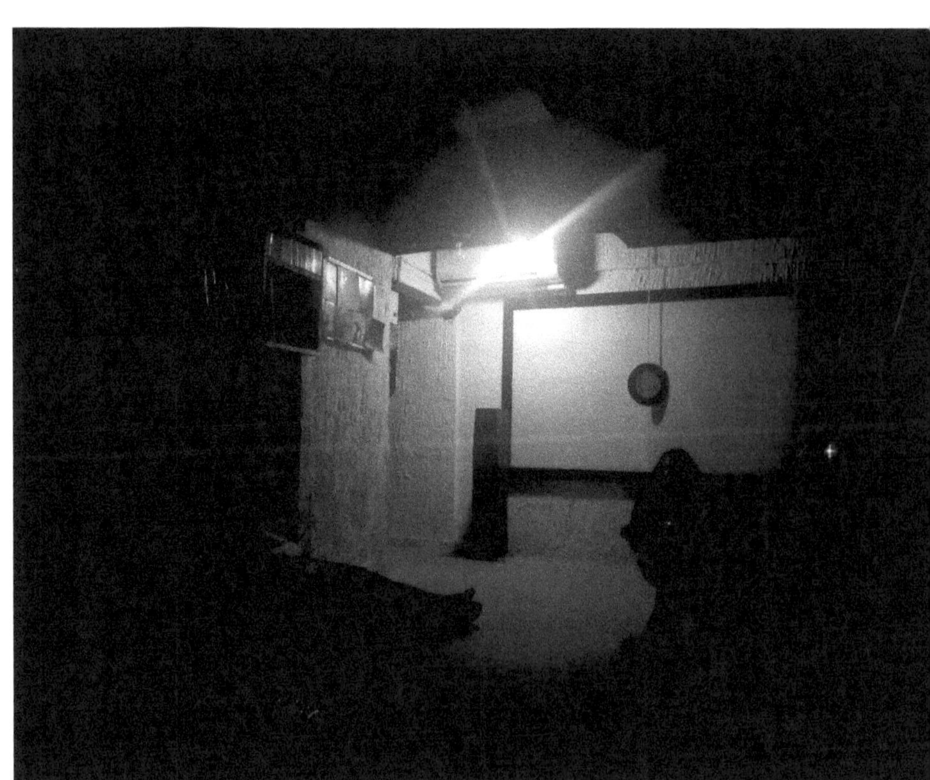

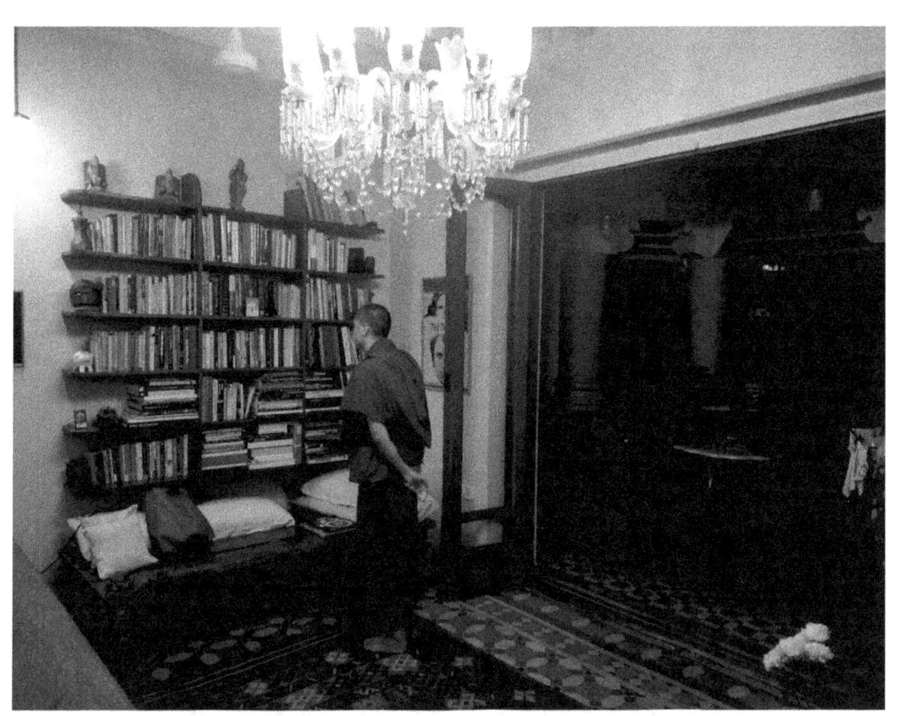

waiting monk
his quietness
speaks with the books

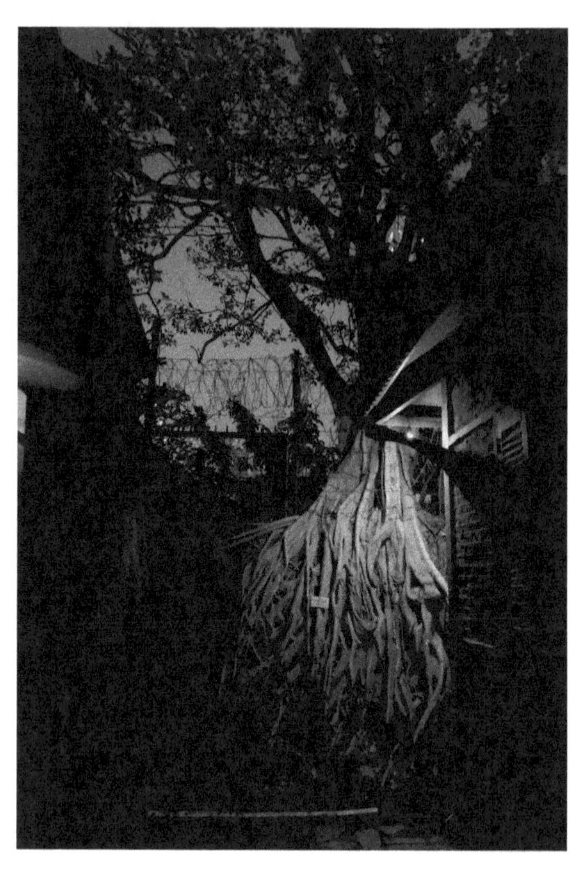

outdoor wall
a banyan shoot curls
in my shadow

evening
a cloud of tobacco
yields a couplet

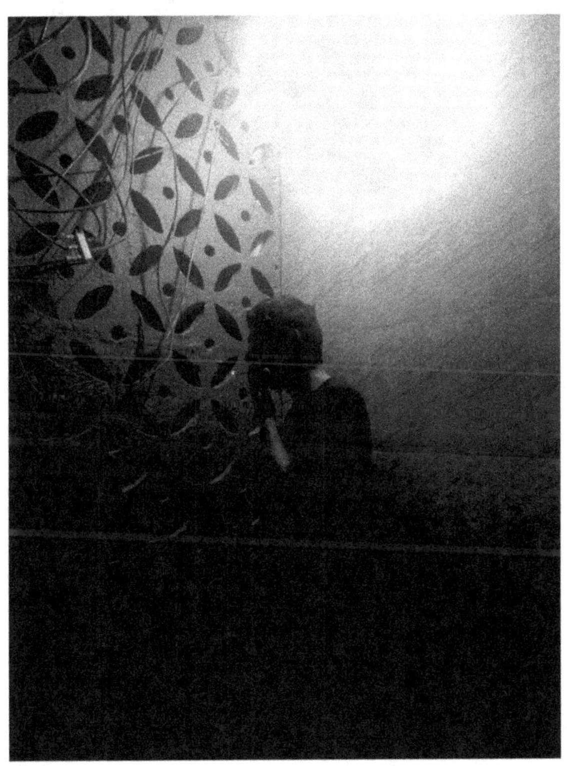

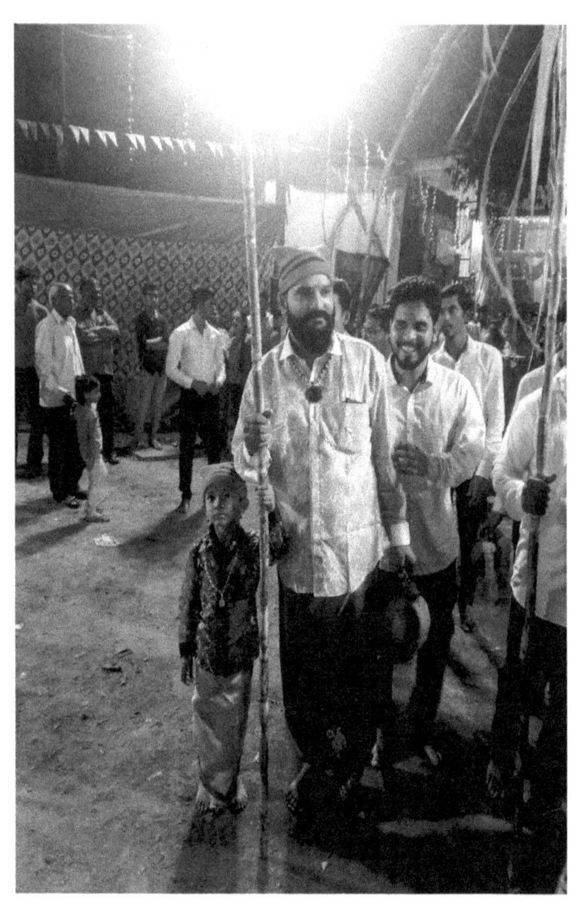

Holi fire
the site
of an absent sea

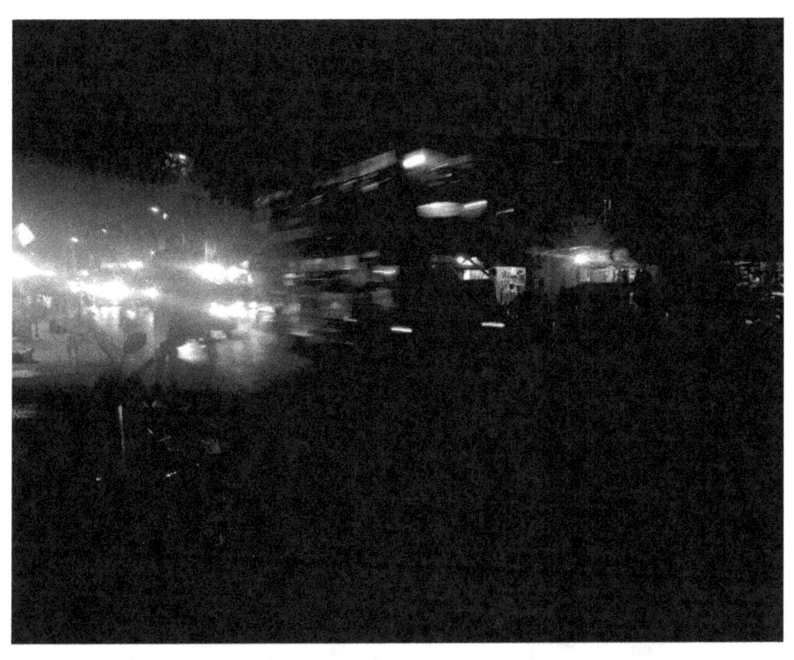

double decker
my childhood self still
in the front seat

midnight
the street dog guards
the woman in the poster

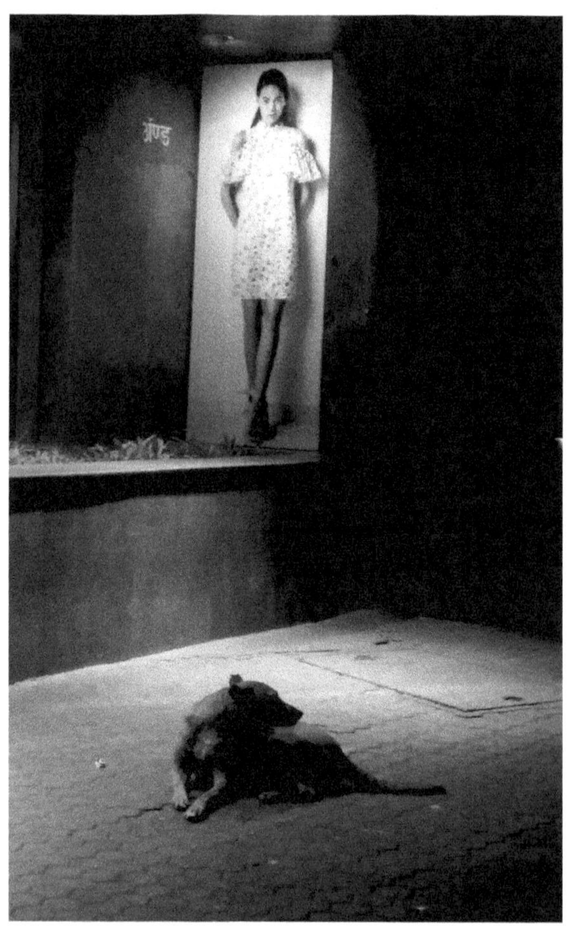

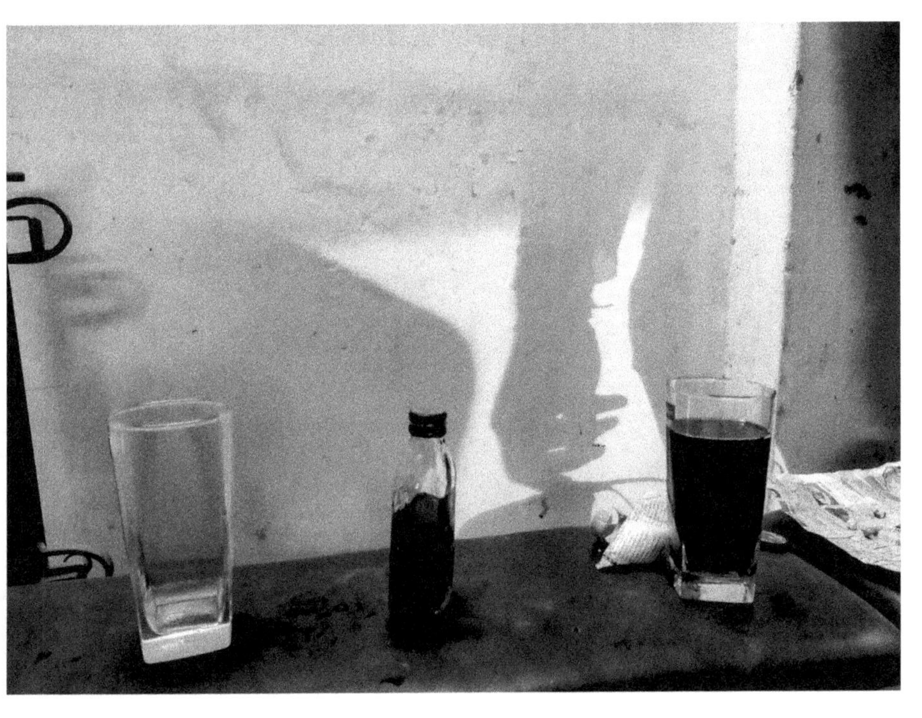

stag party
only cola and rum
date each other

another drink
is the background noise
the sound of time

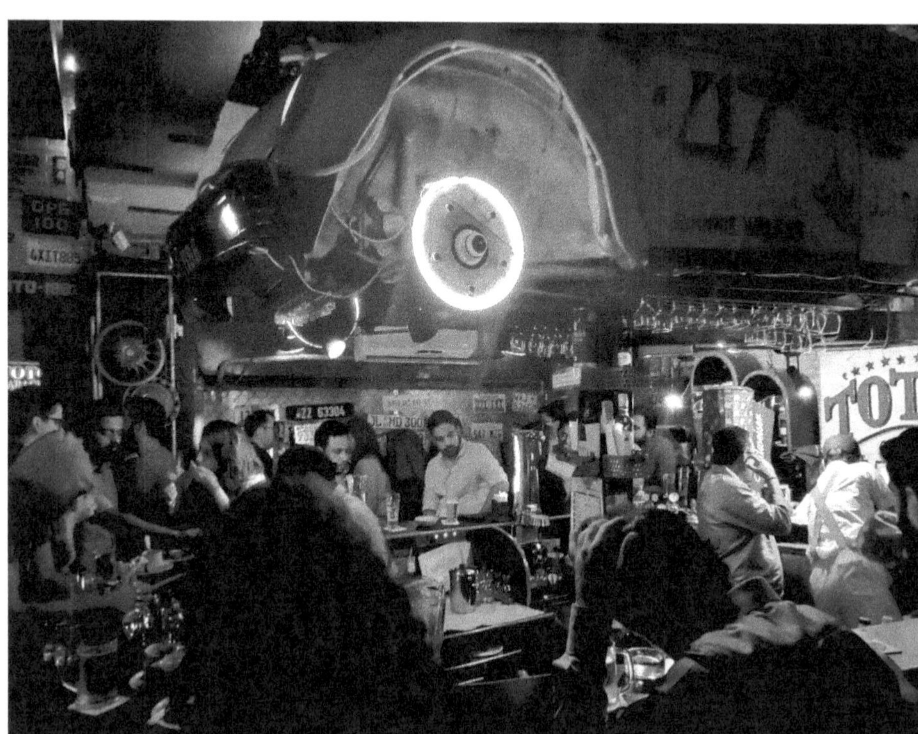

carom pieces
we huddle near
a black hole

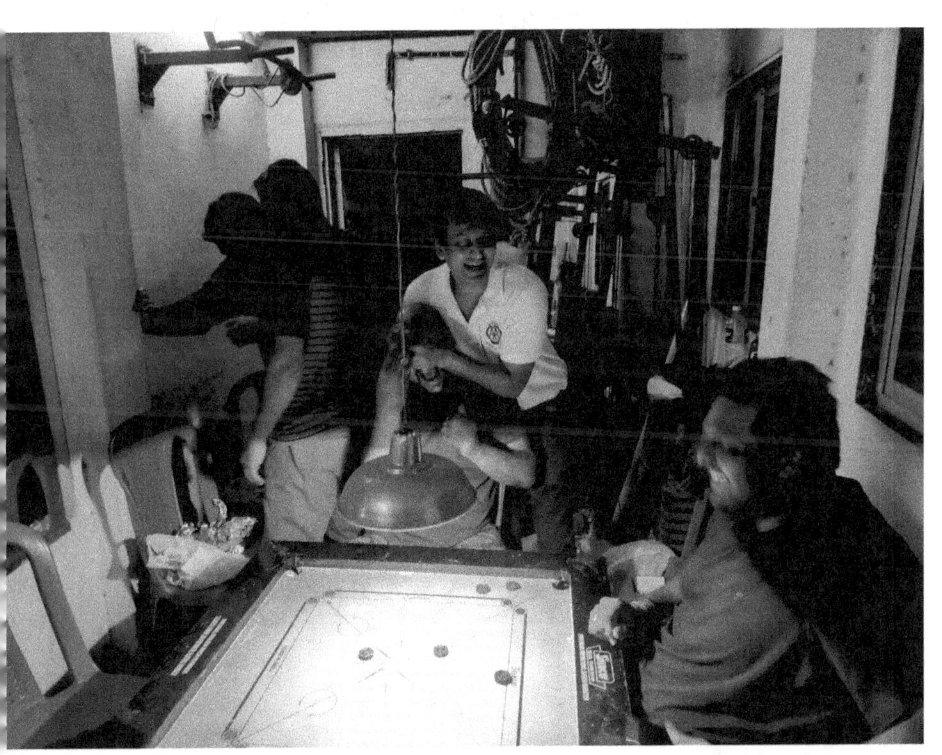

unable to dream
with clocks for eyes
Rajabai tower

a bloodthirsty deity
bedecked
with the skyline

one zero one
yet no dream
zero one zero

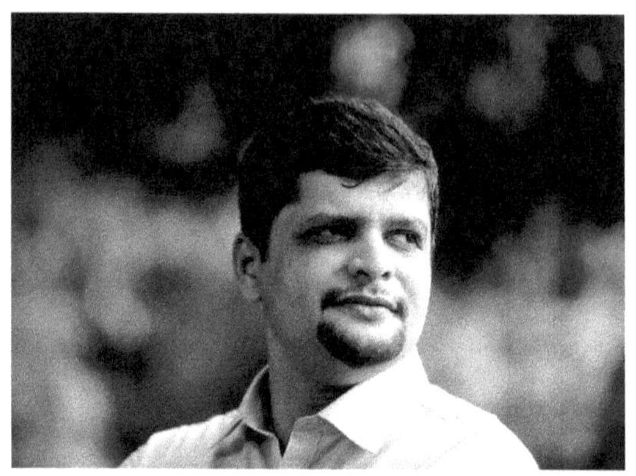

Suhit Kelkar is a poet, journalist, and photographer based in Mumbai. His works have appeared in a number of prestigious publications in India and abroad. Kelkar's first published book was a poetry chapbook called *The Centaur Chronicles* (Hawakal), which deployed the figure of a centaur to explore issues of discrimination and social alienation. *Mumbai Monochrome* is his second book. He is available on Twitter and Instagram: @suhitkelkar.

www.ingramcontent.com/pod-product-compliance
Lightning Source LLC
LaVergne TN
LVHW010254200726
843506LV00014B/3260